Architectural Details *from* Old New England Homes

by Stanley Schuler

Schiffer Publishing Ltd

77 Lower Valley Road, Atglen, PA 19310

Other books by the author

American Barns

The Cape Cod House

Mississippi Valley Architecture: Houses
of the Lower Mississippi Valley)

Old New England Homes

Copyright © 1987 by Stanley Schuler.
Library of Congress Catalog Number: 87-62395.

Printed in the United States of America.

ISBN: 0-7643-0280-7

Published by Schiffer Publishing, Ltd.
77 Lower Valley Road
Atglen, PA 19310
Phone: (610) 593-1777
Fax: (610) 593-2002
E-mail:schifferbk@aol.com
Please write for a free catalog.
This book may be purchased from the publisher.
Please include $2.95 for shipping.
Try your bookstore first.

We are interested in hearing from
authors with book ideas on related subjects.

CONTENTS

Architectural Details
from Old New England Homes

I am just home from a brief expedition through the southeastern Connecticut countryside. The area is growing rapidly, and even on the back-country roads new houses are springing up all over the place. Maybe half of them are of so-called Contemporary design. The rest are good old New England Colonials.

Yes, it is 1987—yet half the houses being built are of early New England design. Not just in southeastern Connecticut. Throughout New England. And to considerable extent in the nearby Middle Atlantic states. I can see my Modern-architect acquaintances shaking their heads in dismayed disbelief. By all rights—considering the fickleness of American taste—we should have given up this archaic architectural style several generations ago. But it is going as strong as ever.

New Englanders—in fact, a good many non-New Englanders—have a love affair with Colonial design (to use the name loosely). We always shall. Why? Because it has such basic appeal. It's like a sculpture by Michelangelo or a painting by Rembrandt. Their styles may no longer be in vogue, but their works are so beautiful that they will live forever. Just so with early New England architecture. We want to perpetuate it. So we build yet

This handsome "old" door is actually just a copy of an old door. It was built about 1930.

another traditional New England house or something very close to it.

Southerners feel much the same way about Southern Colonial design. People in Pennsylvania and surrounding states feel much the same way about their version of Colonial design. But New Englanders are more rabid than all of these.

Early New England architecture has not only made a lasting impression on New Englanders but it also enjoys a unique popularity throughout the country.

I find this a bit difficult to explain.

To most people, all early New England architecture is "Colonial". Actually, in the years from 1630 to 1820 there were four architectural styles in New England. First was the Jacobean or Medieval style that came over with the earliest settlers from England. Then followed the Colonial style (1700 to 1780) and almost simultaneously the more formal Georgian style. And finally (1780-1820) there was the Federal style. (The same four styles in somewhat different versions prevailed in the South and Middle Atlantic regions.)

Whether you call these styles by their right names or lump them all under the heading of Colonial, the houses that were built looked much alike. Popular belief holds that they were very simple, plain, spare, severe. But this description applies only to real Colonial houses (the kind built between about 1700 and 1780). Georgian and Federal houses were more elaborate. So were Jacobean houses, although in a different way.

Be this as it may, all early New England houses were quite simple (although not necessarily plain, spare or severe). They were rectangular in plan; essentially rectangular in elevation. Facades were balanced. Room arrangement was straight-forward. In short, you can look at the houses and instantly understand them. You don't have to spend time figuring how your family can live in them. You don't worry about whether they can be adapted to your way of life because long exposure to old New England houses assures you that they are extremely adaptable. If you're building a new house, you can be reasonably certain that your builder is familiar with the construction and will therefore know how to hold down his costs and your final expenditure.

Old New England houses also have an extremely clean-lined look. Clean lines are an expression of simplicity, and Americans have always liked them because we most certainly are not a complex people. To be sure, there have been times when we took a fancy to tricky or murky lines. We were enthusiastic about Victorian architecture for much of the 19th Century and again in very recent years. But in the long run we always go back to clean, simple early New England architecture.

One other characteristic of New England houses is their reliance on familiar, simple building materials that are employed without any attempt at cuteness. Our ancestors built with only a few materials—wood clapboards for the exterior walls (shingles did not come into widespread use until long after New England was settled), wood shingles for the roof, brick or sometimes stone for the chimney and foundations, wood and plaster indoors—and although this made for a great sameness between houses, the basic effect was restful. In far too many Contemporary houses, by contrast, the exterior is a hodgepodge of materials used in tricky ways that betoken a builder without design judgment or taste. Victorian houses were likely to be guilty of the same fault.

What I am saying here is that simplicity is indeed the primary hallmark of early New England homes and the primary reason why we hold them in such esteem today. However, several additional features help to distinguish the houses from others of the same era and also undoubtedly have contributed to their popularity.

●New England doorways, for one thing, were in a class by themselves. I don't mean to belittle the lovely doorways of Middle Atlantic and Southern homes. But New Englanders put a special emphasis on their doorways. Whether this was because they were friendlier than they are thought to have been and were simply extending a warm welcome to visitors, or whether they were trying to relieve plain, often austere facades with an element of beauty I do not know. Whatever their reasons, they treated their doorways—prominently centered in the facade—as if they were jewels to be cut and polished to capture attention.

●New England chimneys were large—occasionally massive—and generally centered on the ridge of the roof. If you have never thought how much they contribute to the appeal of the houses, take a look at some of the New England houses with wispy little chimneys that were built after about 1840. One is like an athlete in his prime; the other like the same man after he has been hit by a dread disease.

●Saltbox and gambrel roofs were common in New England. Although they were not unknown farther south, they were much less frequently used there.

●When New Englanders began to orna-

The house is an old Federal. The roof balustrades were built of modern materials and added recently.

ment their homes, they favored unusual shapes for dormer roofs and often used two or three different designs on the same house.

•During the Federal period, wealthy New England owners of mansions had a fondness for roof balustrades. Those just below the roof peak—forming what has become known as a captain's or widow's walk—were echoed in houses elsewhere. But balustrades at eaves level were virtually a Yankee trademark.

•Another feature of New England homes was their close affinity with the ground on which they stood. Old Southern homes particularly were built high off the ground. New England homes, on the other hand, hugged the ground.

This is one reason, I believe, why they have special appeal now, when we have a great yen for outdoor living and like to move from indoors to outdoors and back again on one level.

The people who are building traditional New England homes today fall into two categories: those seeking to preserve the past and those that are interested in copying the past.

The preservers are rebuilding or restoring the many houses that have survived from the 17th, 18th and 19th Centuries. Most of these are individual families that acquire ancient houses which they then redo. You can read all about them every month in Colonial Homes, Preservation

The fireplace at the bottom of this page, left, has an antique mantel bought in an antiques store for a new house. The other mantels are new—built by carpenters with stock materials or materials made to order by local wood-working firms.

News, Old House Journal and other publications. Others, less numerous, are builders like my young friend Harry "Skip" Broom. Skip has for some time been restoring old houses for clients and building new ones to look exactly like the old. Now, having more or less exhausted the local supply of antique dwellings, he is searching throughout New England for houses that he can purchase, take apart, move and rebuild on land he owns in southeastern Connecticut. Such is the demand for these buildings—which like most antique houses are modernized inside and sometimes enlarged—that he even employs a person to scout out houses that have been overlooked because they are in decaying downtown sections of early mill towns.

The copiers of traditional New England homes are, of course, far more numerous than the preservers. Generally, they are leery of owning a real antique house either because they fear it will develop dreadful physical problems such as a severe case of rot or because they do not want or do not see how to make a compromise between the small rooms, small

8

windows, thin walls and other characteristics of old homes and modern equipment, living habits and desires; nevertheless, they are so captivated by the architecture of the past that they want to build new houses in the same style. Some of these people, like my friends the Schwartzes, go to considerable lengths to build houses that are, at least on the surface, so faithful to the past that you think they actually came out of the past.

Others—especially those that value modern features as highly as the antique look—put up houses that are merely suggestive of the past. My wife and I built two such houses some years ago. One that we built for ourselves was to the passing glance an oversize Cape Cod Colonial. The other, built on speculation so we could control what went up on the lot next door, was advertised as a Deerfield Colonial. No one that knew early New

England architecture would have thought either house was old; but thanks to a very capable architect and our own knowledge and feelings about such things, the houses expressed the feeling of old New England.

Countless houses of the same kind are a-building today. The famous old architectural firm of Royal Barry Wills & Associates has been directly responsible for scores of them and indirectly responsible for thousands more that were copied from Mr. Wills' plans and books. In recent years, developers here and there around New England have been building them hand over fist. Even the prefabbers have gotten into the act. From Bow House, Inc., for instance, you can buy semi-prefabricated story-and-a-half Capes that look much like the Jabez Wilder house that was built in Hingham, Massachusetts in about 1670.

It makes no difference whether you're an old house preserver or copier—if you're thinking about acquiring an attractive genuine or imitation old New England home, you must be conversant with early New England architectural styles.

Many people seem to feel that if they are familiar with the overall appearance of the old houses, that is enough. But such is not the case. To capture the full flavor of the past in a house, you must also be familiar with the way individual parts of the house are designed. That's the reason for this book.

My previous book, *Old New England Homes*, was a largely pictorial review of all the house styles that prevailed in New England from 1630 to 1900. The pictures, for the most part, showed New England homes in their entirety—as they are seen from the street.

In the book you now hold, the entire emphasis is on the doors, walls, roofs, windows, fireplaces, stairs and other specific architectural details of houses that were built before 1820, the date generally considered to mark the starting point of the Greek Revival style of architecture—our first truly national style of architecture. I do not pretend that the pictures here illustrate every variation of every early architectural feature. They are merely representative. But I believe you will find among them examples that you can use in your own home or adapt to it.

I should like to think that this book—augmented perhaps by my previous book—is all you need to design the house you're dreaming of. But it is more than likely that you will need some of the following sources of information and inspiration in addition.

1. A great many books have been published about early New England houses. The fact that most are old and most are concerned more with the general appearance and plan of houses than with architectural details does not negate their value. You should certainly look for them in your local libarary.

2. The only magazine that concentrates on early domestic architecture is Colonial Homes. It does not cover New England houses in every issue, but it covers them often and beautifully. I recommend it highly.

3. Many of the architectural details contributing to the beauty of Georgian and Federal houses in early New England were taken by the early builders from books they imported from England. Copies of these, unfortunately, are scarce—to be found only in a few large libraries. But the books of Asher Benjamin, a famous and very influential Massachusetts builder, were reissued by Da Capo Press several years ago and are more widely available. You should study these for specific details that you might like to duplicate.

4. An even better (because it's more varied) source of measured drawings is the Historic American Buildings Survey (HABS) collection of documents stored in the Library of Congress. These documents, which include photographs as

Interior and exterior of the large living room that Connecticut builder Skip Broom added to the 18th Century Georgian house he bought and restored for himself. Because he's in the business of restoring early New England homes, Skip picks up and reuses a lot of antique moldings, mantels, etc. But the huge Palladian window and practically all the fine woodwork in this room were specially made to Skip's order by local craftsmen.

well as superb architectural drawings, show floor plans, elevations, fireplaces, corner cupboards, doors, windows, moldings, hardware, etc. of thousands of early American homes, many of which have been destroyed. (I have incorporated about a dozen sheets of HABS drawings in the pages that follow.)

To study these drawings you must pay a visit to the Library of Congress yourself. Then, having found the details, plans, etc, that you want to work from, you can order photocopies from the Library's Prints & Photographs Division.

5. Equally valuable information is to be had by looking at houses surviving from the past and touring some of those that are open to the public. In New England, you don't have to go far to find innumerable architectural gems, because they are everywhere. But they are, of course, especially plentiful in certain communities such as Salem, Massachusetts; Newport; Cambridge; the hill section of Providence; the area between Mt. Vernon Street and the Boston Common; Portsmouth; Newburyport; Castleton, Vermont; Wiscasset and Guilford.

Taking the time to go through old houses that are regularly open for viewing is particularly worthwhile because it's the only way you can study the interior details. Furthermore, the guides that lead you through the houses are sufficiently steeped in architectural lore to point out and discuss features that are typical as well as atypical of houses of the same era.

A partial list of houses open to the public on a regular basis is given on Pages 175-176. Most of these houses are open daily but only in late spring, summer and early fall. You must check with their owners for dates, times and admission fees. Of the many houses that are pictured in the pages following, the only ones that are fully identified are those that you can visit.

6. Once you reach the point where you're about ready to start actual planning of your new home or remodeling, you must decide who is going to do the work. Of your four choices, only one is good.

You can try doing it yourself. But don't. The job requires far more knowledge, skill and patience than most laymen have.

You can turn to a building contractor. But don't. Contractors may know how to construct buildings but, despite their claims, this does not give them the ability to do the kind of skilled planning you want.

You can buy a plan from Colonial Homes or one of the several magazines on the newstands that sell house plans. Such plans, naturally, are usable only if you're building a house, not if you're remodeling. But I advise against them. The sketches illustrating the houses are misleading. Neither the designs nor the plans are very good. And if you want to alter them, you must find somebody who can do the work because the original architect won't.

You can hire an architect. This is the only course of action you should take. To be sure, not all architects are expert or even moderately proficient in the design of New England Colonial, Georgian or Federal homes; and even those that do have a good feel for these styles are not necessarily fine architects. Even so, because of their long education and training, architects will come closer to designing a good house—quite possibly a superlative house—than anyone else. Although they add to the cost of your project, the work they do more than justifies their fees.

You should not, however, engage just any architect. Check out several who are recommended to you by home owners whose judgment you trust. Then talk with the architects at length about themselves, yourself and your family, and the kind of house you want. Inspect other

Early Cape Cod houses often had bowed roofs, so Bow House, Inc., now sells plans and materials for building excellent, roomy modern bowed-roof Capes like this one.

houses—particularly traditional houses—they have built. Then and only then should you make your choice.

But don't stop at that. Even though you have no design skill yourself, don't quietly accept everything your architect recommends. If you don't think that what he has done is correct in every way, say so. After all, you're paying the bill, so you are the one to be satisfied. Don't, however, be adamant in your opinion of how a feature of your house should be designed because you might be wrong. I know of a man who hired a topnotch traditional architect to design a replica of an old New England home and who then insisted that all the windows should have single panes. The architect, a tactful fellow, managed to "forget" the order every time it was given until finally the client realized that he was very wrong.

There are three mistakes that Americans who build or remodel traditional homes frequently make if they have not familiarized themselves with early New England architecture and/or if they fail to hire a competent architect:

1. They do not understand what makes the architectural details they are trying to duplicate attractive and effective and they therefore botch the copy they make. I have in mind the scroll pediment above the front door of a house in my com-

The rooftop balustrade and corner pilasters were built with standard building materials.

munity. As the pictures on pages 96-102 show, the scroll pediments used on antique doorways were magnificent, rather complex things; but anyone who studies them casually may conclude that they are easily reproduced. At least that is what the owner of this particular house concluded because he ended up with the sorriest imitation of a scroll pediment I have ever seen. If I were to picture it, you would see instantly what is wrong with it (and I'd be sued by the owner for defamation). It is like a scrawny picked chicken; too small, too flat, too angular, too characterless.

Many, many other replicas of other architectural features are equally poor—all because the designer or owner or whoever was responsible for them did not fully appreciate the original he was copying.

2. Too often a fine architectural detail is imposed on a house without any regard for what the house looks like. For instance, few people are seriously offended by a simple Colonial cupboard in a Contemporary house. But try using quoins on a Contemporary house.

3. Home owners often do not see or understand the relationship—sometimes subtle; sometimes quite obvious—between design features and the rest of the structure. Here's a case in point: A young couple came before my town's historic district commission, of which I'm a member, to get approval of the house they hoped to build in the district. They had drawn up the plans themselves with the advice of their contractor—a very poor combination of talents—but they had done a surprisingly good job. The house was a large Georgian. But while the commission approved it in overall, we felt there were several small things that should be changed. One of these was the fanlight in the gable facing the street. It just wasn't right for the triangular space surrounding it. "But," they protested," it's exactly like the window in the so-and-so house" (one of our town's most admired old Georgians). "That may be," I said, "but it's still wrong. Take a look at the so-and-so house again."

Actually, I myself wasn't certain exactly what was wrong with their fanlight; but when I passed by the house they were copying from, I saw at once that it had a much flatter roof than the house they had planned and the fanlight was therefore rather flat (to be specific, it was segmental rather than semi-circular).

Happily, when the young couple took a second look at the so-and-so house, they came to the same conclusion: they had to give their fanlight a higher arch to make it relate comfortably to the gable of their house. (PS. In similar fashion, they corrected the other minor flaws the com-mission had noted and now the house is under construction. It will not be a perfect 18th Century Georgian when completed but it will be a very satisfactory replica.)

This was, of course, an isolated incident. Many towns do not have historic district commissions; and even in those that do, the commissions have jurisdiction only over the buildings in a designated historic area—not over those in the entire town. Furthermore, almost no towns have architectural review boards with authority to approve or disapprove everything that is built in the entire community. Consequently, very few people can count on having an unbiased, knowledgeable outsider tell them whether the house they hope to build is architecturally right or wrong.

But there are many other things you can do to help yourself, as pointed out earlier.

The final task in building a new old house or remodeling a true antique may at first seem more impossible and discouraging than any part of the planning process: Where do you find the materials to execute the architectural details your blueprints call for?

Actually, because of mounting interest in preserving our architectural heritage, the job is probably easier today than it was twenty-five years ago. Even so, you may have to do a certain amount of frantic searching for materials like those that were required to complete the doorways, fireplaces, etc., that are illustrated in these opening pages. Yes, the features pictured are all new. I include them so you can see that what you can't get one way you can get in another.

Some early architectural details can be duplicated with stock materials available from any building supplies outlet. The roof-top balustrade on the opposite page and the corner boards on the same house are cases in point. both were fashioned out of ordinary lumber.

Other common early features are available as stock items from companies that produce special building supplies. For example, the Morgan Company in Oshkosh, Wisconsin turns out a full line of mantels, cabinets, stair railings, etc. in traditional designs. Similarly, Driwood Mouldings in Florence, South Carolina, produces and sells accurate reproductions of practically every period molding, chair rail, window casing, etc. that was ever used. There are numerous firms like these; but if you can't locate one that sells the particular items you need, you can undoubtedly turn to a local woodworking firm that will make them for you. The mantel and surrounding paneling on Page 9 came from sources of this kind.

Honest-to-goodness antique materials are available from large junkyards as well as small companies and individuals that collect and store them in anticipation of the time that somebody like you will come asking for them. The fine Federal mantel on Page 8, for example, was purchased from a New York City store specializing in antique fireplaces, mantels and related items.

Finally, if all other sources of supply fail you, don't overlook the possibility of finding a craftsman who can make for you an excellent copy of anything that was made before—even such things as the extremely ornate mantels and balusters of the Georgian period. For example, the magnificent doorway on Page 4 is so expertly crafted that I thought—as everyone else does—that it was made 200 years ago. Instead it is the handwork of a modern-day woodworker. Similarly, every stitch of woodwork in the handsome "old" living room on Page 11 was made in a modern woodworking shop.

It will be many, many years before any "old" New England homes that you and I and others build today develop the lovely patina of age we see in the houses built by our ancestors in the 17th, 18th and 19th Centuries. But if we design them carefully, following ancient models, and build them carefully, they will probably be as much admired and copied in the 22nd Century as the originals are now.

New England "Colonial" goes on forever.

16

Saltbox roofs, like that on the Thomas Griswold House in Guilford, Conn., were a New England characteristic and very common in the Colonial period. The gambrel roof was also popular, but unlike the Newport house at left, most houses had roofs with double pitches on both sides of the ridge.

Roofs

COLLECTIONS OF THE LIBRARY OF CONGRESS

The 1694 section of the Hale House in Beverly, Mass. (opposite) has a gable roof; the wing added in the 1700s, a gambrel roof. Above is the Jabez Wilder House (not open to the public). Like many early Cape Cod-design houses, it has a bow roof. At right is the John Ward house in Salem, Mass. Its steep roof is broken by two cross gables. These were common in homes of Jacobean design.

ESSEX INSTITUTE, SALEM, MASS.

19

Hip roofs like that on the King Caesar House in Duxbury, Mass. (opposite, top) were especially common on Federal houses. On the Newport house opposite, bottom, the very upper part of the hip roof is shaped like a gable roof with very little pitch and runs lengthwise of the roof. Roof balustrades adorned many of the great Georgian and Federal houses. In both cases here, the roofs are hipped, but the roof above has a double pitch and is known as a mansard. The pedimented, slightly projecting section of the facade is called a pavilion.

M.C. WALLO

New Englanders often built balustrades at the eaves as well as near the roof peak, and some houses had balustrades at both levels. The latter is true of the Peirce-Nichols House (right, top) and the Andrew-Safford House (right, bottom), in Salem, Mass. (Both balustrades are visible in the picture of the Safford House.) Balustrade designs varied considerably. In the Georgian period, balusters were arranged more or less in a row broken only by newel posts. But in the Federal period, solid panels were often sandwiched between groups of balusters as above and right.

23

Balustrades were used on gambrel roofs as well as hips, and if used near the peak of the roof, they varied widely in size. The brick house at left is the McClellan-Sweat House in Portland. At the top of this page is the Hunter house in Newport. The post detailed above is on the Hunter House.

For many, many years after the Pilgrims landed, New England chimneys were usually centered on the roof and very large. Most of them were square and plain, like that of the Saconesset Homestead, West Falmouth, Mass. (left). But it was not unusual for the chimney to be ornamented with pilaster-like projections as on the Cooper-Frost-Austin House, Cambridge (bottom, far left), the Howland House, Plymouth (opposite, bottom right) and the Eleazar Arnold House, Lincoln, R.I. (two pictures below).

The placement of chimneys at or near the ends of a house came into fashion with the Georgian architectural style. Long before that, however, a few houses in or near Rhode Island had end chimneys. These houses were called stone-enders, because the chimney and surrounding masonry wall took up one entire end wall, or the better part of it. The Arnold House is an example. In the Hart House, Old Saybrook, Conn. (right), just a small part of the chimney shows through the end wall.

On these pages are two more pilastered chimneys. The roof of the Wanton-Lyman-Hazard House in Newport (right) kicks out at the bottom and overhangs an unusual coved plaster cornice. Three methods of covering exterior walls are illustrated by the three pictures below. On the blue house, graduated clapboards are used on the facade. The center house is clad with rusticated wood siding using wide boards deeply chamfered along the edges and at intervals up and down to resemble carefully cut stone. Beaded siding is used at far right.

Graduated siding has always been something of a mystery and no one has explained exactly why clapboards were handled in this way—with the lowest boards having an exposure of two inches or less and the upper boards having an exposure of about four inches. But the scheme must have been solely for decorative purposes because it was, as a rule, used only on the facade. The other walls were clapboarded or shingled in normal manner.

Overhangs

In England upper walls that overhung those below served a practical purpose although we're not certain what it was. In America some of the houses built in the later 1600s had overhangs on the front and/or sides, but apparently they were strictly decorative. If the overhangs were about a foot deep, they were usually adorned with drops and brackets as on the Stanley Whitman House, Farmington, Conn. (left, top) and Parson Capen House, Topsfield, Mass. (left, bottom). Connecticut overhangs (this page) were usually shallower and unornamented.

At right are brackets on the Deacon John Grave House, Madison, Conn., and the Buttolph-Williams House, Wethersfield, Conn. (two pictures at far right). Such brackets are less important than the overhangs, which evidently were used only to create a pronounced horizontal line that would make a house look longer and less tall than it actually was. Subsequently, horizontality was established in other ways. In the house at left, for instance, the builder used a slightly projecting string course of bricks across the front and sides. In the house opposite, at top, the cornice was continued across the gable end to form a large crowning pediment. In the Gore House in Waltham, Mass. (above) the cornice just turns the corner and stops; but the gable is separated from the wall below by a board.

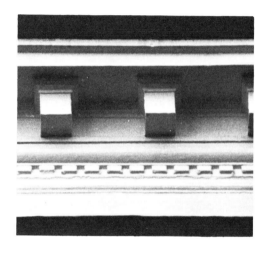

Georgian ornament of home exteriors was more exuberant than Federal. On the facing page are several examples. The garlands and festoons applied to Federal friezes (this page) were especially delicate and lovely, but they are much more common in Vermont than other New England states.

The standard way to trim a house, particularly of Georgian design, was with rows of big, spaced blocks called modillions and rectangular teeth called dentils. It was also a fairly common practice to drill shallow holes in patterns in moldings and mutules (flat blocks like those at far left, bottom). Today, many of these trim pieces must be made to order. But modillions (note that there are two designs) and dentils are available from stock.

35

The better New England houses of the 18th and early 19th Centuries often made use of the old Greek and Roman orders. For instance, the columns and entablature of the portico on this Vermont house are essentially Doric (even when American builders used an ancient order they did not necessarily follow the design slavishly). The frieze below the cornice repeats the frieze of the entablature. The clusters of little vertical strips are triglyphs.

Corners of houses were treated in different ways. On modest Colonial houses, they were normally covered on both sides with flat boards to which the siding was butted. Board width varied but averaged about six inches. On large houses corner treatment was more elaborate. Handsome pilasters similar to those on the facing page were often used.

The alternative to corner boards and pilasters was quoins. At first glance they all look very much alike, but if you examine the three above, you will find that they are not. In some cases, short blocks on both sides of the corner alternated with long blocks. In other cases, each set of blocks consisted of a long piece and a short piece; and the long pieces ran lengthwise of the facade at one level and lengthwise of the end of the house on the next level. In addition, block sizes varied from one installation to another.

Illustrated on the facing page are two typical window arrangements. On large three and four-story Federal houses like that at bottom, first-floor windows are tallest, second-story windows are shorter, top-story windows are shorter still. In Cape Cod houses the second-story windows in the gable ends are erratically placed. The arrangement shown is common, but sometimes there's a fifth window at the roof peak; sometimes the small windows are quarter-rounds; sometimes there is only one large window; and so on.

Windows

Above is another Cape Cod house with another arrangement of gable windows. At far right is a four-story city house with graduated windows. The ground-floor windows are short because that floor was used more for working purposes than the second floor, which has floor-to-ceiling windows so people could step from the living room, etc., out onto small balconies.

Another characteristic of the largest Georgian houses was variation in the window and door heads. Quite understandably, these differed from house to house. More than that, they differed from floor to floor in the same house and between doors and windows. The center house, top, is the Moffatt-Ladd House in Portsmouth; the yellow house below it is the John Paul Jones House, also in Portsmouth.

Very early houses had small diamond-shaped panes in leaded casements. Rectangular panes in lead followed. Then came double-hung wood sash. In the Colonial/Georgian period the muntins were thick, as here. In Federal windows they were slender. Opposite are assorted window heads. Despite general similarity, all are different.

More kinds of window head. The simple treatment used on the Jeremiah Lee House in Marblehead, (left) is common. Note that the flat white lintel is flush with the siding; the keystone projects slightly. Sometimes the lintel projects as much as two inches, and frequently the keystone is missing. The Lee, Wells-Thorn House (below left), Hatheway House (below), Dwight-Barnard House (opposite, lower right) and Codman House next to it are open to the public.

44

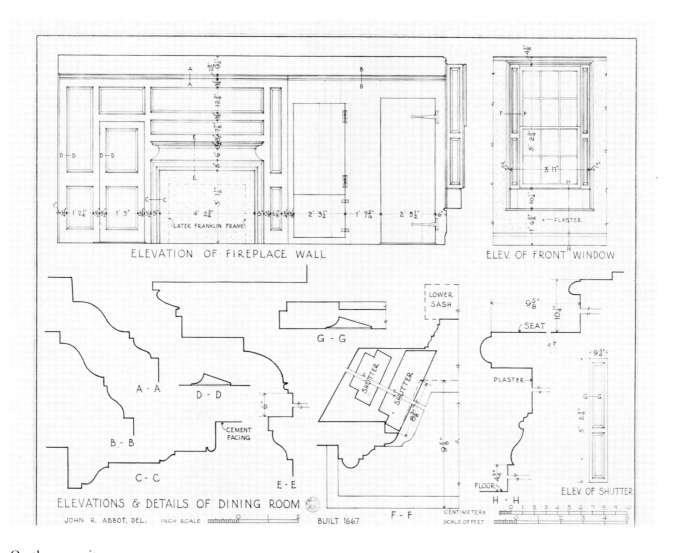

ELEVATION OF FIREPLACE WALL

ELEV. OF FRONT WINDOW

LATER FRANKLIN FRAME

A - A

D - D

B - B

C - C

E - E

CEMENT FACING

G - G

LOWER SASH

SHUTTER

SHUTTER

SEAT

PLASTER

FLOOR

ELEV. OF SHUTTER

H - H

F - F

ELEVATIONS & DETAILS OF DINING ROOM

JOHN R. ABBOT, DEL.   INCH SCALE   0   1   2   BUILT 1667

CENTIMETERS   0 1 2 3 4 5 6 7 8 9 10
SCALE OF FEET   0   1   2   3   4   5

On the opposite page are still more window treatments. The large picture at top illustrates a treatment popularized by the great Boston architect, Charles Bulfinch, who liked to recess windows slightly in blind arches. The picture at right is of the Derby House in Salem, Mass. The windows have paneled inside shutters that fold into the walls, as in the plan above. Surprisingly, inside shutters used to be more common than outside shutters. The latter were not widely used till about the middle 1700s.

Care must be taken in selecting a gable window to make sure it is compatible in size and shape with the roof slope and pediment, if any. The yellow house (top) is the Florence Griswold House in Old Lyme, Conn. Below it at left is the Salisbury Mansion in Worcester. At right is the Cowles House in Farmington, Conn. (closed to public). The facade is dominated by the Palladian window and gorgeous entrance with Ionic columns.

48

Triple windows

Although the Palladian window is generally considered the most beautiful of residential windows, similar three and four-sash windows can also be very handsome. The two on this page are examples. The window above simply repeats the design of the doorway. The one at right looks like a Palladian but the semi-circular top is not glazed. A typical Palladian window is shown at far left. That to the immediate left is also a Palladian but has unusually narrow side sash. Furthermore, Palladian windows are rarely recessed in a square wall panel.

The Palladian window came into use in the United States just before 1750. It was usually made the central feature of the facade—just above the front door—and served to light the stairway. But variants of the window soon appeared. These became especially popular in the Federal period. The window above is in a Connecticut house built in 1798. The same window is shown at top, right on the facing page.

Except for the Palladian window in the gable of a very simple Colonial home at right, all the windows on these pages are from the Federal period. The beautiful window above was, of course, designed to match the adjacent doorway. Simple three-unit rectangular windows like the two at the bottom of the opposite page often took the place of Palladian windows in Federal houses.

Although Palladian windows are generally associated with mansions like the Andrew-Safford house in Salem, Mass. (above), the Codman House in Lincoln, Mass. (above right), the Nickells-Sortwell House in Wiscasset, Me. (far upper right) and the private house in Litchfield, Conn. (upper left, facing page), they are easily adapted to much smaller houses like the other two shown.

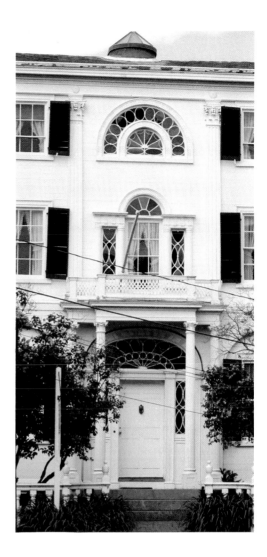

The John Brown House (left) and the Ives House (bottom left) are two of the country's great mansions. Both are in Providence on the same street. Both have extraordinary Palladian windows above the entrance portico. Below is a much simpler window that is unusual because it's in a dormer and because the two side windows are only about half the height of the central unit.

The most common form of dormer has always been a rectangular window under a gable roof. But on large New England dwellings, the dormers often were given other shapes, and frequently two different shapes were used on the same roof slope or on adjacent slopes on the same house, as on the facing page.

The roofs of the dormers on the two houses on the opposite page are much larger than the bodies of the dormers and suggest a colonial general wearing a three-cornered hat. The house at top is the Hamilton House in Berwick, Me.; below it is the Gov. John Langdon House in Portsmouth. Note the Chinese Chippendale roof balustrade and the ornate corner pilasters of the latter. The two-window dormer at right is not to be outdone in beauty by either the Langdon or Hamilton dormers. The house above is in Newport, where numerous houses have dormers of similar design.

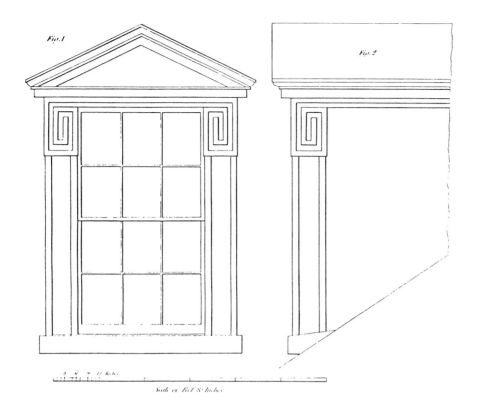

Fig. 1

Fig. 2

Asher Benjamin was a Massachusetts builder whose books greatly influenced house design in the early 1800s. At left is one of his suggestions for a dormer. It is reprinted here from the DaCapo Press edition of Benjamin's books. Below: Round-headed windows were sometimes used toward the end of the 18th Century. Opposite is a typically beautiful New England doorway.

Doorways

Even casual study of the pictures on the next fifty pages teaches several things about the front doorways of old New England homes:

1. Visually, they were the most important single element of a house. Except on half and three-quarter houses, they were almost always centered in the facade. They were never hidden—the stranger never had to hunt for them as he does when approaching many modern homes. In Georgian and Federal mansions they were even centered in a pavilion which was in turn centered in the facade. (A pavilion is a slightly projecting section of the front wall that extends to the eaves and is surmounted by a pediment. See large picture on Page 80.)

2. The beauty of the doorway was in the surround, or enframement. In this respect, old doorways were quite unlike the modern doorway, which usually depends for whatever beauty it has on the door itself. Very old New England doors were plank doors. Those that followed were simple paneled doors—generally six-panel doors.

3. Front doors always opened into a hall—not into the living room as is so often the case (unfortunate) today.

Next to the plain board-framed doorways of the simplest Colonial houses, doorways with triangular pediments were probably most popular in early New England. The doorways on these two pages are all in the College Hill section of Providence, but similar doorways are to be seen everywhere. Most date from the 1700s and have semi-circular fanlights. The window above the door at left is entrancing—one of a kind. Note that the tracery in the arch repeats that in the doorway's fanlight.

Double doors were reasonably common on New England houses after about 1730. Nobody knows quite why, but it was probably because they made for a wider and therefore more imposing entrance. Many people use them today for the same reason. But double doors have a practical disadvantage that even our very practical ancestors ignored: each door panel is usually so narrow that you have to edge your way through when only one door is open— and it is not often that both panels are open. The doors of the Sheldon-Hawks House in Deerfield (far right, top) are especially narrow—only 21 inches. At right is the Deming-Standish House (1790) in Wethersfield, Conn. It's now a restaurant.

If you don't want to try reproducing an old doorway, there is a very good chance that you can find someone who has an actual antique doorway to sell you. The doorway at far right, for instance, dates from 1759. The house itself was built in 1830.

For many years, New England entrances were flat in the facade. They gave no protection from rain and snow when you stood outside; they opened directly into the cramped front hall. Change came sometime in the 1700s. To increase hall space, houses acquired vestibules as at left and above. Or to keep rain off callers, doors were put under porticoes or hoods as on the Boston houses at right.

74

On the opposite page are three old houses with vestibules that in all cases were added after the house was built. Doorways in vestibules are rarely as attractive as those under porticoes and they obviously don't keep water from the roof from drowning visitors. But they do increase floor space and, if big enough, may provide a needed coat-hanging space. At left is the Stanton House in Clinton, Conn; above it, the Webb House in Wethersfield, Conn. On the facing page, bottom right, is the Hooper-Lee-Nichols House in Cambridge.

Every once in a while "conservative" Yankees went a little wild. The Newburyport portico (above left) and the fancy hood over the Newport entrance (facing page, bottom) are examples. But as the other doorways show, even when early home owners and builders were being typically conservative, they took great pains to make their entrances beautiful.

The doorway at left is in the the same yellow house as the doorway on the preceding page. Compare them. Then compare them with the doorways on the facing page. Across the bottom of these pages are three similar porticoes.

It was noted earlier that contractors should not be trusted to design an early New England home. This is especially true if you plan to protect your front entrance with a columned portico because the columns are very difficult to design. Prefabricated aluminum columns—the kind most builders automatically select—are unsatisfactory because, unlike those illustrated here, they do not have entasis. Entasis is defined as the slight convex curving of the sides of a tapered column that should be used to eliminate the optical illusion of concavity characteristic of straight-sided columns. The untutored may think this a very unimportant, picky point; but it's one of the main reasons why old columned porticoes are so handsome. The top, right house on the facing page is the Gardner-White-Pingree House in Salem, Mass. Below it is the Peirce-Nichols House, also in Salem. The Ives House in Providence is immediately to the left.

The recessed doorway above is on Mt. Vernon Street in Boston. City doorways were often recessed; country doorways were not.

Flat-topped doorways often have a rather monumental look. This is especially true of those at left and right and others like them, so if you choose a design of this kind, you must make sure the doorway does not overwhelm the house. On the other hand, flat-topped doorways have a practical advantage: they are easier for a good home handyman to build than many other types of doorway.

The flat-topped doorways on this page are less imposing than those on the preceding pages. That above is in the Welles-Shipman-Ward House in South Glastonbury, Conn. The doorway at top right on the facing page is sort of midway between the two styles. The other doorways on the facing page are much simpler. The flat, heavy ledge resting on brackets is called a console. The design appears a bit gawky, but it was quite popular in the past, especially in Providence.

Sidelights bordering flat-topped doorways tend to be narrow. In the doorway at far left, louvered panels replace sidelights. The transom is interesting because it is wider than the door but does not fill the space between the brackets. On this page are three simple doorways in brick walls. That in the Asa Stebbins House in Deerfield (below) is edged with raised brick panels. The odd doorway in the Merwin House in Stockbridge, Mass. (below right) has been turned into a window but retains its original appearance. Other more conventional doorways in brick houses are shown on Pages 79 and 81.

On these pages and the three following are close-ups of doorheads that grace New England's early houses. Study them closely. No two are exactly alike. They range from rather simple, as at left, to extremely complex, as above. Some have fanlights or transoms or sidelights; others are totally without glass. (The choice depends on whether you need more natural daylight in the front hall.) But all are certain to invite the attention of the passerby and give a cordial welcome to the visitor.

91

Except for the doorway with a wood fan spanning two doors (to a two-family house), the doorways on the facing page are exceptionally ornate. They contrast sharply with the very simple Colonial doorways on this page. Earliest doors were like the nail-studded plank door on the Eleazar Arnold House in Lincoln, R.I. (below). They were set in the plainest possible kind of wood frame. Later doors, whether double or single, were set in wider board frames and almost always were surmounted by transoms. The top casing often had flared ends.

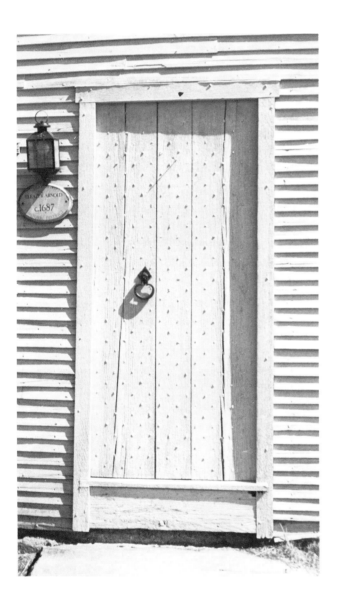

Except for the unusual two-panel door (most doors had six panels), the doorway above is like those on roughly five out of ten houses of Colonial and Cape Cod design. And as in most of the early Colonial and Cape Cod houses, the doorhead is close under the eaves (windowheads are also close under the eaves). The effect is simple, yet oddly attractive. However, many early-18th Century home owners became dissatisfied with so much simplicity and replaced the plain casings with something a bit fancier— such as the pilasters on the other doorways illustrated. The doorway on the facing page, left, is in the Atwood House in Chatham, Mass.

Three photos: COLLECTIONS OF THE LIBRARY OF CONGRESS

Most magnificent of the early doorways were those with a broken pediment. This is the kind that many modern home owners try to copy—with disastrous results. This does not mean that a highly skilled craftsman cannot turn out an excellent replica. But the pediment, whether scroll-shaped as here or segmental as at right, must be designed with utmost care and executed in the same way.

The Connecticut River Valley doorway on this page is relatively simple—especially in contrast to that of the Hunter House in Newport (opposite page). Both feature a pineapple between the rosettes at the very peak of the pediment because the pineapple is the symbol of hospitality. However, mushrooms and other objects were also used as models for doorway finials.

96

Above is another Newport doorway. It is within stone's throw of the Hunter House and looks so much like it that you immediately think they are twins. But there are definite differences in the base of the pediment and below.

At right are two pictures of the great doorway in the Parson Ashley House in Deerfield. It, too, has a pineapple betwen the rosettes, but the fruit is small and very stylized. The double doors with old bullseye glass are almost as handsome as the surround. As in most scroll pediment doorways, the double doors are of special design.

On the next three pages are three more scroll-pediment doorways. The Dwight-Barnard House doorway in Deerfield is on Page 100; the Babcock-Smith doorway in Westerly, R.I. is on Page 102.

The most elaborate of all scroll pediment doorways is in the Metropolitan Museum of Art in New York City. The Museum of Fine Arts in Boston has two fine doorways.

Segmental-pediment doorways—so called because the pediment is an arch forming less than a semicircle—were less common than other doorway designs and usually quite simple, like the above and that on the preceding page. However, the doorway on the opposite page is anything but simple. Today, unhappily, it is in rundown condition.

The doorway at right and above right is in the Longfellow House in Cambridge. The house is magnificent but not pretentious and the console-topped doorway is quite in keeping with it. Note also that the doorway is in perfect scale with the pavilion in which it is set and the entire facade. This is the first requirement of a good doorway.

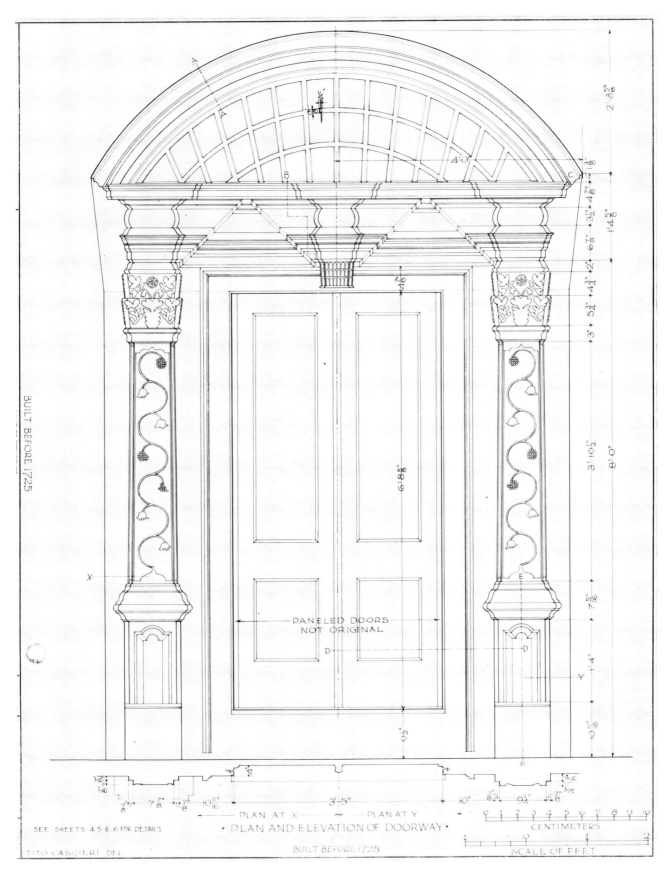

PANELED DOORS
NOT ORIGINAL

BUILT BEFORE 1725

SEE SHEETS 4·5 & 6 FOR DETAILS

TITO CASCIERI DEL.

PLAN AT X — PLAN AT Y
· PLAN AND ELEVATION OF DOORWAY ·

BUILT BEFORE 1725

CENTIMETERS

SCALE OF FEET

It's generally said that you can recognize a Federal house by the doorway, which has a graceful fanlight as well as sidelights. This is true but ignores the fact that a few Georgian houses had fanlights and sidelights. Furthermore, some Federal houses had fanlights but not sidelights. So don't be surprised to find that a few of the doorways in the next several pages are not of the Federal period.

Be this as it may, doorways of this type are exceedingly lovely. Quite gentle and charming in contrast to the gorgeous but somewhat heavy doorways of the Georgian era (such as those on preceding pages). Here are three examples. They are not necessarily the prettiest doorways to be found in New England, but they are very satisfying.

The doorway on the facing page is in the Florence Griswold House in Old Lyme, Conn.

In the doorway above the elliptical fanlight is framed by an intricate border of rosettes and diamonds that are in turn framed by a fine bead molding. The muntins in the fanlight spring from a sunburst. The doorway, top right, is equally unusual because of its massive frame of cut-stone slabs. The windows are similarly framed. Square-headed doorways like this came into use in the very early 1800s and became common during the Greek Revival period starting about 1820.

Up until about 1800 fan-
lights were semi-circular, as
at left. Then elliptical or
segmental fanlights came
in. In Georgian fanlights
the muntins were made of
wood. Leaded glass was
made popular by the Adam
brothers, the great English
designers responsible for
the Federal architectural
style. Many of these
windows are incredibly
delicate in appearance.
They can be duplicated
today only by the most
skilful craftsmen.

109

The two houses at right (top and bottom) are Georgian; the other three, Federal. The doorways make this clear. There is a delicacy about the Federal designs that the Georgian doorways don't have. However, the monumental doorway of the first Harrison Gray Otis House in Boston (below) is something of a borderline case.

The doorway at left is a special charmer. It is in Castleton, Vt. Castleton is populated with a most unusual collection of houses designed by Thomas R. Dake, an architect with a mind of his own.

As shown on earlier pages, wood fans were occasionally substituted for fanlights. These are easier to duplicate today than the leaded glass of the Federal period but they don't have the same advantage over the simpler fanlights of the Georgian period. The head of the doorway (top, far right) is shown in close-up alongside. Soon after the doorway was constructed in Providence in 1824, a neighbor a block away copied it exactly. Above is the lovely entrance to an old house on the Connecticut River. The door itself is new.

...evably
...eled
...emselves
...he main
...built in
...ational
...ook an
...e delicate
...in the
...very
...equally
...re strips
...effect is

SCHIFFER PUBLISHING LTD
77 LOWER VALLEY RD
ATGLEN PA 19310-9717

PLACE
STAMP
HERE

Stairs in Jacobean and early Colonial houses were built around the central chimney and were very steep. Balusters were usually turned; otherwise, stairs were plain. Scrolled end blocks below the treads, as at left, were unusual. A few stairwells had a candle shelf, as at bottom of page.

The odd stairway shown in the two pictures above is sometimes called a "Good Morning" stairs. From the front door, it rises straight up for a few steps, then divides and rises the rest of the way in two flights. Shutting off a stairway with a door, as in the Atwood House in Chatham, Mass., was done to conserve heat, but it is a dangerous practice. The entry and stairs in the ancient Lee House in South Lyme, Conn., are in the middle of the opposite page.

The Buttolph-Williams House in Wethersfield, Conn., dates from 1692 but is like the Jacobean houses built much earlier. The stairway (three pictures) is in a narrow entry. It's very steep, unusually wide and has terrible winders. The banisters above the plain board-paneled wall are only about a foot high. (Those in other early houses are equally short.) The rail against the chimney wall of the stairwell was installed recently to protect vistors.

The large picture at far right was taken in another Connecticut house built in 1754. It gives a good idea of how narrow entries were in early houses. In contrast to the Buttolph-Williams House, the wall below the stairway is nicely paneled, the banisters are taller.

On Page 121 is the stairway in the Hunter House in Newport. (Photo from the Preservation Society of Newport County.) On Page 120 is a Salem stairway of the same vintage. (Photo from the Essex Institute.) Note the handsomely paneled ceiling under the upper flight in the Hunter House.

Georgian stairways are notable for several reasons: (1) In the big, expensive homes, balusters and newel posts were intricately turned, as on the facing page. (At top left is the Derby House in Salem, Mass.; at top right, the Webb House in Wethersfield, Conn.) (2) Balusters of three different designs were placed on each tread; and the turned part of all three began at the same height (in other words, the turnings were unequal in length). (3) The ends of the steps, which were exposed, were paneled (as at lower left, facing page) or covered with scroll work (top right). (4) The railings, instead of connecting directly to the newel posts, were connected with curved easings (as in the Hart House in Old Saybrook, Conn., above). This gives the railings a sort of swooping look that is very graceful.

Some of these ideas were retained in the Federal period, but as noted previously, banisters then were generally much simpler. The banisters in the Peirce-Nichols House in Salem are shown at bottom right on the facing page. This house, designed by Samuel McIntire, was originally Georgian, but McIntire remodeled the interior in the Federal style.

On the two pages following are several more Federal-style stairways. No architectural feature is so breathtaking as a circular staircase such as these. That in the Gore House, which was designed by Charles Bulfinch and built in Waltham, Mass., is particularly beautiful and unbelievable. It is shown on Page 124 and the top of 125.

Three photos: ESSEX INSTITUTE, SALEM, MASS.

Four photos: ESSEX INSTITUTE, SALEM, MASS.

125

Above is one of the stairs in the Hatheway House, Suffield, Conn. At right is the short flight in the front hall of the Wentworth-Coolidge House near Portsmouth. The newel post of the former is made of four balusters tightly clustered—a unique idea. At top right is the typically steep stairway of a Colonial dwelling.

Interior walls

126

Wainscots were common in New England homes in the 18th Century. Two often-used types are shown on these pages—those with recessed panels, as at right and far left, and those with raised panels, as in Newport's Hunter House (below) and at the left in the Wentworth-Coolidge House. (The board paneling above the wainscot in the house at right is a recent addition and a sad mistake.) Arches—handsome or otherwise—like that in the Hunter House were uncommon in early New England.

Plain vertical board paneling pretty much like
that so widely used today was fairly common in
early New England houses; but when
Americans began to take time to beautify their
homes, the paneling they installed was made up
of wide boards with chamfered edges set in a
framework of rails and stiles and often separated
by pilasters. Though each paneled wall had its
own look, there actually was not a great deal of
difference in the paneling except on the chimney breasts. One paneling design, however, was
unique. This was known as tombstone paneling
for the obvious reason that the panels were
shaped like tombstones, as at left. Tombstone
paneling was probably the fanciest paneling
produced by our ancestors.

Above is one of the rooms in the Peirce-Nichols House in Salem, Mass. The paneled walls are sub-servient to the mantel, the doorheads and the cornice moldings. The overmantel paneling, although simple, is lovely enough to be displayed as here. But it could also serve as a fine background for a painting.

Opposite is the tombstone paneling in the dining room of a Connecticut house built about 1740. The whole house is now undergoing extensive renovation. The paneling here looks scruffy because it had to be completely disassembled, scraped and put back together again in a tight fit. The lighter colored wood by the mantel and in the cornice is new. One of the interesting things about the wall is that the pilaster to the left of the fireplace is a good inch wider than that to the right. Notice how much the cornice overhangs the wall. Notice, too, that the summer beam is paneled. The wall paneling will eventually be painted.

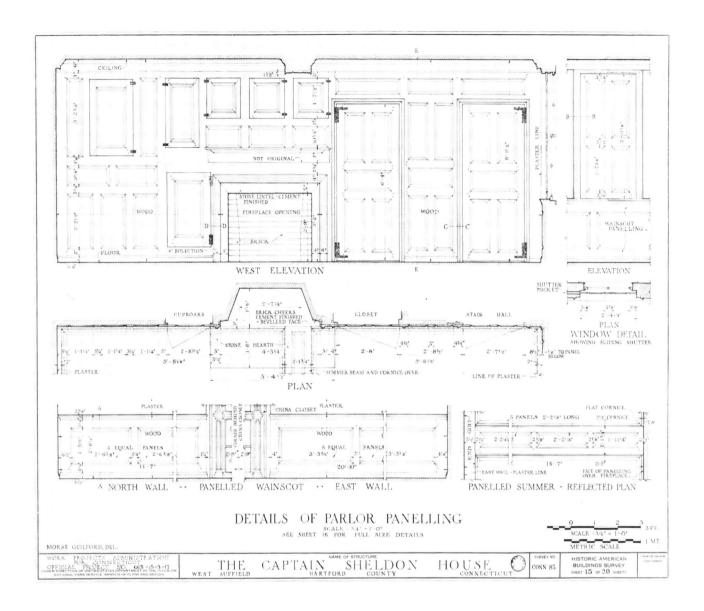

DETAILS OF PARLOR PANELLING

SCALE 3/4" = 1'-0"
SEE SHEET 16 FOR FULL SIZE DETAILS

WEST ELEVATION

PLAN

A NORTH WALL · PANELLED WAINSCOT · EAST WALL

PANELLED SUMMER · REFLECTED PLAN

ELEVATION

PLAN
WINDOW DETAIL
SHOWING SLIDING SHUTTER

MORSE GUILFORD, DEL.

| WORK PROJECTS ADMINISTRATION FOR CONNECTICUT OFFICIAL PROJECT NO. 665-15-3-17 UNDER DIRECTION OF UNITED STATES DEPARTMENT OF THE INTERIOR NATIONAL PARK SERVICE, BRANCH OF PLANS AND DESIGN | NAME OF STRUCTURE THE CAPTAIN SHELDON HOUSE WEST SUFFIELD HARTFORD COUNTY CONNECTICUT | SURVEY NO. CONN 85 | HISTORIC AMERICAN BUILDINGS SURVEY SHEET 15 OF 20 SHEETS |

You don't necessarily need an architect to design the paneling for a wall if you can find in the drawings made for the Historic American Buildings Survey the kind of paneling you want. The HABS drawings, like those above, are superbly detailed—all a good craftsman needs to work from. But unfortunately, they will not answer the question of where will you find boards in great enough widths for panels like those pictured at right. Such boards just don't exist today unless they are salvaged from buildings that have been torn down. You may have to use hardwood plywood instead.

Two photos: COLLECTIONS OF THE LIBRARY OF CONGRESS

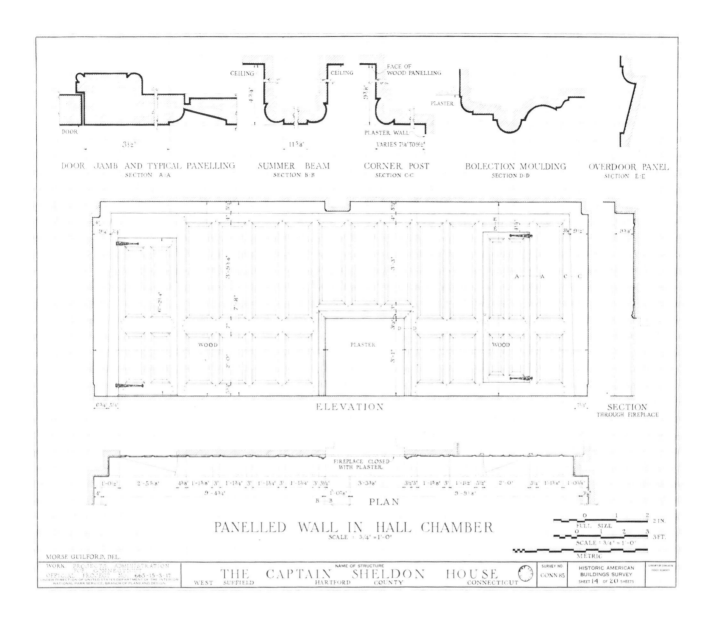

DOOR JAMB AND TYPICAL PANELLING
SECTION A-A

SUMMER BEAM
SECTION B-B

CORNER POST
SECTION C-C

BOLECTION MOULDING
SECTION D-D

OVERDOOR PANEL
SECTION E-E

WOOD

PLASTER

WOOD

ELEVATION

SECTION
THROUGH FIREPLACE

FIREPLACE CLOSED
WITH PLASTER

PLAN

PANELLED WALL IN HALL CHAMBER
SCALE : 3/4" = 1'-0"

FULL SIZE
SCALE : 3/4" = 1'-0"
METRIC

MORSE GUILFORD, DEL.

WORK PROJECTS ADMINISTRATION
FOR CONNECTICUT
OFFICIAL PROJECT NO. 665-15-3-17
UNDER DIRECTION OF UNITED STATES DEPARTMENT OF THE INTERIOR
NATIONAL PARK SERVICE, BRANCH OF PLANS AND DESIGN

NAME OF STRUCTURE
THE CAPTAIN SHELDON HOUSE
WEST SUFFIELD   HARTFORD   COUNTY   CONNECTICUT

SURVEY NO.
CONN 85

HISTORIC AMERICAN
BUILDINGS SURVEY
SHEET 14 OF 20 SHEETS

133

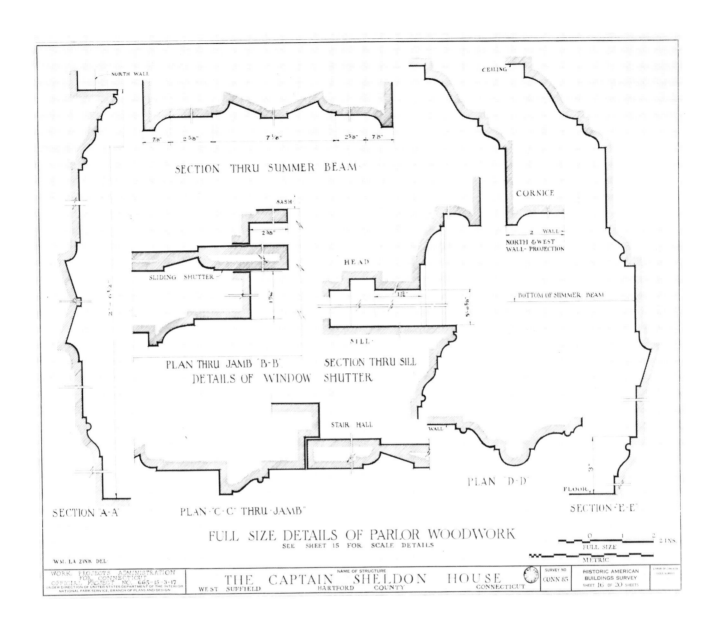

NORTH WALL

7·8" 2·5/8" 7·1/8" 2·5/8" 7·8"

SECTION THRU SUMMER BEAM

CEILING

CORNICE

2 WALL

NORTH & WEST
WALL- PROJECTION

BOTTOM OF SUMMER BEAM

SASH

2·3/8"

SLIDING SHUTTER

PLAN THRU JAMB "B-B"
DETAILS OF WINDOW

HEAD

1·1/2"

SILL

SECTION THRU SILL
SHUTTER

STAIR HALL

WALL

PLAN "C-C" THRU "JAMB"

PLAN "D-D"

SECTION "A-A"

FLOOR

SECTION "E-E"

FULL SIZE DETAILS OF PARLOR WOODWORK
SEE SHEET 15 FOR SCALE DETAILS

0   1   2 2 INS.
FULL SIZE
METRIC

WM. LA ZINK DEL.

WORK PROJECTS ADMINISTRATION
FOR CONNECTICUT
OFFICIAL PROJECT NO. 665-15-3-17
UNDER DIRECTION OF UNITED STATES DEPARTMENT OF THE INTERIOR
NATIONAL PARK SERVICE, BRANCH OF PLANS AND DESIGN

NAME OF STRUCTURE
THE CAPTAIN SHELDON HOUSE
WEST SUFFIELD   HARTFORD COUNTY   CONNECTICUT

SURVEY NO
CONN 85

HISTORIC AMERICAN
BUILDINGS SURVEY
SHEET 16 OF 20 SHEETS

This sheet of HABS drawings gives further details of the paneling detailed on Page 132. The photos at left and above right show a much simpler and earlier form of paneling, but even it would confound a good many modern carpenters who tried to copy it. Below right is an unusual paneled wall in the Stanton House in Clinton, Conn. It divides the parlor from the front hall. The wall dividing the hall on the far side from the dining room is similar. Both walls are hinged so that they could be swung up against the ceiling when the Stantons needed a ballroom.

If you work too hard to remove paint, nail holes and other defects from old board paneling, you end up with handsome panels that have little character. It's often better to remove just the worst of time's ravages and let matters take their course. Actually, the paneling at left is more attractive than this harshly lit photo suggests. It is a very dark brown.

The pilasters in the paneled wall of the Hatheway House, Suffield, Conn. (left) were designed as an integral part of the mantel. Rooms in small pictures on facing page are in the Stanton House, Clinton, Conn. Above is the parlor of the Longfellow House in Cambridge. Note particularly the paneled alcove. Alcoves (not necessarily paneled) were rather common in big houses, especially in the Federal era. They usually were designed for the specific purpose of recessing a sideboard, bed or other furniture piece.

Fireplaces

Two beautiful fireplaces—one Colonial, the other Georgian. The width of the panels above the former is unbelievable in today's world. The ornate detailing of the mantel and overmantel of the latter, which is in the dining room of the Hatheway House, in Suffield, Conn., is equally unbelievable. But gorgeous wood and magnificent craftsmanship are par for the course in old New England homes.

Most people seem to think of New England fireplaces as being unusual. Actually, in size and appearance they were not. They were different from other early American fireplaces only in that in most houses they were built around a central chimney.

Be this as it may, old New England fireplaces and their surrounds are well worth duplicating; and the easiest way to do this is to buy a mantel that has been salvaged from a house that's been demolished. This course is, in fact, almost essential if you want a complicated design such as here. Simpler designs can be managed by any good craftsman using stock moldings or reproductions of antique moldings.

The Hatheway House in Suffield, Conn. is one of the most beautiful in New England. Of Georgian design, it was built in two sections. The fireplaces on these pages (the two photos on this page are of the same parlor fireplace) are in the newer part of the house, dating from 1794. The wallpapers are the original French papers.

At left is a detail of the enormous mantel in the Wentworth-Coolidge House near Portsmouth. The fireplace is one of the handsomest and most ornate in the U.S. But other fireplaces in the house (small pictures, right) are more ordinary. Above is a portion of a Federal mantel. The design is no less intricate than that opposite but more delicate.

143

The fireplace at left and right is in the dining room of a house that was falling apart when purchased several years ago. You can imagine the work involved in removing countless coats of paint from the trim—especially from the unusual teeth at the top of the pilasters. The rest of the house was restored in similar painstaking manner. Below is a bedroom fireplace in the Longfellow House, Cambridge. Early fireplace openings were often trimmed with imported tiles.

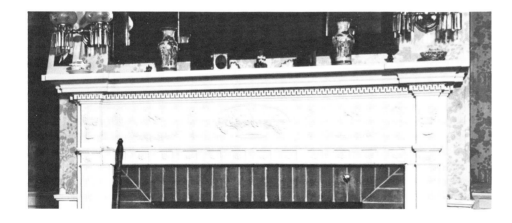

Beehive ovens in the earliest fireplaces were in the back of the fire-box, as at far left, bottom. Then they were moved to the side of the fireplace, as at top, opposite page. Above is a fireplace in the Gard-ner-White-Pingree House in Salem, Mass.

Two fireplaces in the ancient Buttolph-Williams House in Wethersfield, Conn. Both are very big but that was necessary because the rooms they had to heat are big. The enormous molding framing the fireplace at right is a bolection molding. Many early fireplaces were trimmed with the same kind of molding. The mantel shelves for both of these fireplaces are shallow and plain.

149

One way to give prominence to a fireplace without making it overly ornate is to treat the wall around it all the way up to the ceiling—or not too far below the ceiling—as a unit. Consider the fireplaces above and on the facing page. Then compare them with the fireplaces in the small pictures. The corner fireplace with the arched top is in a bedroom of the Hart House in Old Saybrook, Conn. Other arched fireplaces are on Pages 128 and 129.

Three fireplaces from the Amasa Day House in Moodus, Conn. The house was built in 1816, near the end of the Federal period; but the people in this rural area were way behind the times, very simple and conservative, and they designed accordingly. Result: a blend of the Federal and Colonial styles.

Cupboards

The northeast parlor of the Hunter House, built in Newport in 1768. Despite the grandeur of the room, the fireplace treatment is simple. The opening of the firebox is trimmed only with a bolection molding. The pilasters, cornice and shell-topped cupboard are something else again. The windows have inside blinds that fold into the walls.

A former owner of the house at left was so enamored of the old cupboards that whenever he moved (which he did frequently), he pulled them out of the wall and took them with him. The fireplace is not old. Below is an infinitely simpler cupboard.

Interior trim

The cornice in the Hatheway House, Suffield, Conn. (above) looks much like that in the Longfellow House, Cambridge (far right, bottom) until you examine them closely. The decoration of the window apron (opposite, top and middle) is so pretty that the difficulties of painting and cleaning it (and removing old paint later) can be cheerfully ignored. The massive oak summer beam in the Buttolph-Williams House, Wethersfield, Conn. (opposite page) has chamfered corners, and the chamfers are brought to an attractive termination just before the beam meets the girts on which it rests. This mildly decorative treatment of summers came into style in the early 1700s.

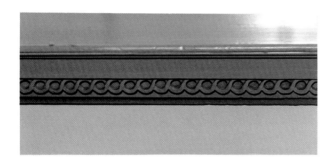

Interior doors

Plain board casings framed most interior doors, but in big houses the treatment—especially of the doorheads—was often pretty fancy, as in the Hathaway House in Suffield, Conn. (left, below left and right). In Georgian and Federal architecture, six or eight-panel doors (below left) were just like modern doors. But Colonial doors were thinner and more variable. Three styles are shown. There were more.

Here are three Federal period doorways in Salem houses. That on the opposite page was designed by Salem's favorite-son architect, Samuel McIntire. The doorway at left is in the Gardner-White-Pingree House.

Left: An inside doorway. Lower left: Back of the front door in the Peirce-Nichols House in Salem, Mass. Below: Front door of the first Harrison Gray Otis House, Boston. At right are some of Asher Benjamin's suggestions for the decoration of architraves (ornamental moldings around the faces of the jambs and lintel of a doorway or window opening). The drawings are reproduced from the 1973-74 DaCapa Press reprints of Benjamin's books.

Two photos: ESSEX INSTITUTE, SALEM, MASS.

SPNEA—J. DAVID BOHL.

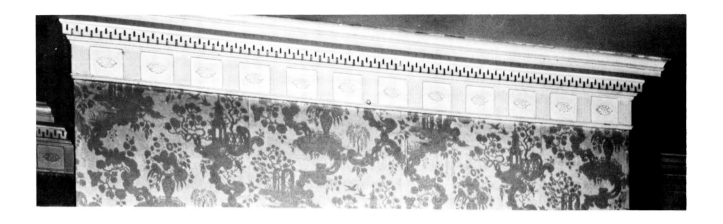

The exposed corner posts in early houses were usually left unadorned but in the Hatheway House in Suffield, Conn., they were covered and treated as handsome pilasters (opposite page). Covering summer beams with panels carved in geometric patterns (above) was a more common practice. Ceiling centerpieces as at left were rare in New England. But fine cornices like that above and on numerous other pages were very popular.

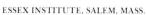

ESSEX INSTITUTE, SALEM, MASS.

Early New England homes lacked closets but were well supplied with cupboards of various sizes and shapes tucked into whatever empty spaces were available. The main cupboard—there was usually only one—was the corner cupboard, known as the ''buffet''. It was customarily built into the parlor against an outside wall. But since it was semi-circular in plan and rather shallow, it might be recessed in a flat wall, usually alongside the fireplace as above and on Pages 154-157.

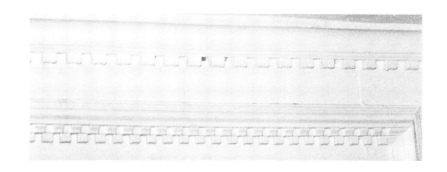

Generally corner cupboards ran from floor to ceiling and were divided into an upper part and smaller lower part. In early cupboards, the top part was sometimes open; usually it had doors with small glass panes. The bottom part had wood doors. The top of the upper cupboard might be a half dome; it was rarely shell-shaped. The entire cupboard was treated decoratively though never as elaborately as a parlor fireplace. Above is one of the cherubs on the cupboard in the Hunter House (Pages 154-155). At left and top is the cupboard in the Stanton House, Clinton, Conn.

169

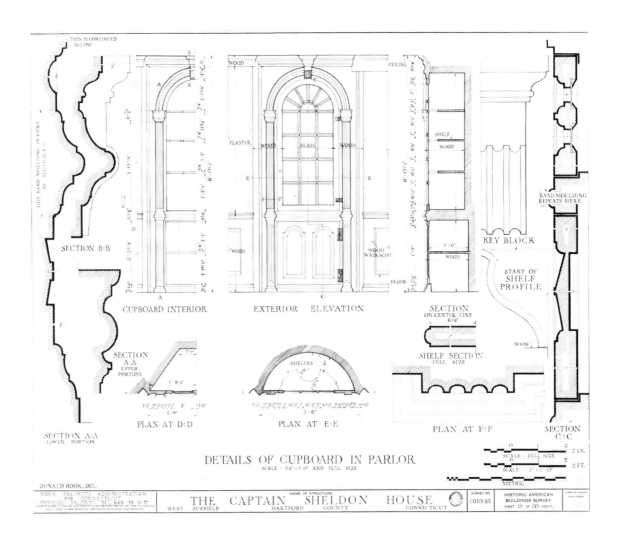

THIS IS CONTINUED BELOW

THIS BAND MOULDING OCCURS AT SECTION C.C

SECTION B:B

SECTION A:A UPPER PORTION

SECTION A:A LOWER PORTION

CUPBOARD INTERIOR

PLAN AT D:D

WOOD

PLASTER WOOD GLASS WOOD

WOOD

WOOD WAINSCOT

FLOOR

EXTERIOR ELEVATION

SHELVES

PLAN AT E:E

CEILING

SHELF

WOOD

1-6"

WOOD

SECTION ON CENTER LINE

SHELF SECTION FULL SIZE

PLAN AT F:F

KEY BLOCK

BAND MOULDING REPEATS HERE

START OF SHELF PROFILE

DOOR

SECTION C:C

DETAILS OF CUPBOARD IN PARLOR
SCALE : 3/4"=1'-0" AND FULL SIZE

DONALD ROOK, DEL.

SCALE : FULL SIZE

SCALE : 1"=1'-0"

METRIC

The cupboards in the HABS drawings are of better design than most cupboards were. Few, however, were as plain as that at far right, bottom. The cupboard at left is in the Hart House, Old Saybrook, Conn.

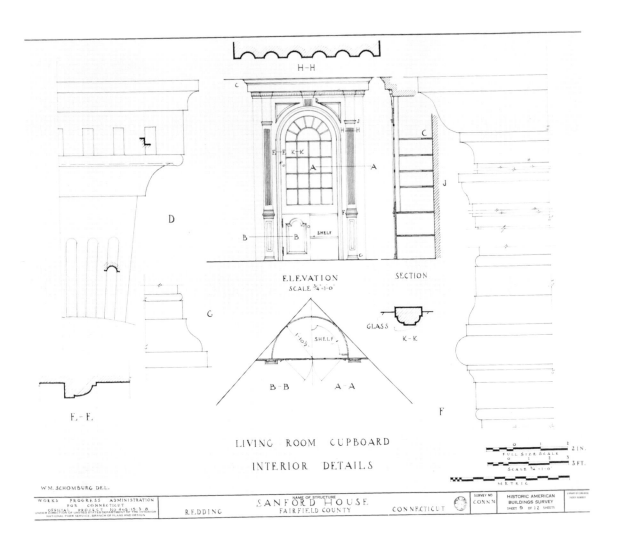

H-H

ELEVATION
SCALE 3/4"=1'-0"

SECTION

GLASS

K-K

D

B SHELF

B-B   A-A

SHELF

E-E

G

F

LIVING ROOM CUPBOARD

INTERIOR DETAILS

W.M. SCHOMBURG DEL.

FULL SIZE SCALE   2 IN.
SCALE 3/4"=1'-0"   3 FT.
METRIC

WORKS   PROGRESS   ADMINISTRATION
FOR   CONNECTICUT
OFFICIAL   PROJECT   NO 665 15 3 8
UNDER DIRECTION OF UNITED STATES DEPARTMENT OF THE INTERIOR
NATIONAL PARK SERVICE, BRANCH OF PLANS AND DESIGN

REDDING

NAME OF STRUCTURE
SANFORD HOUSE
FAIRFIELD COUNTY

CONNECTICUT

SURVEY NO.
CONN 74

HISTORIC AMERICAN
BUILDINGS SURVEY
SHEET 9 OF 12 SHEETS

ESSEX INSTITUTE, SALEM, MASS.

Above and below: COLLECTIONS OF THE LIBRARY OF CONGRESS

The HABS drawings on the next two pages give you only a small idea of the hardware our ancestors used. For a more complete idea, you must pore through many more HABS files. There is no museum of antique hardware; no publication covering it thoroughly. But there are craftsmen here and there who can make copies of antique hardware to order. Several hardware manufacturers offer copies of a few old hinges, pulls, etc. as stock items.

At left is the corner cupboard in the Atwood House, Chatham, Mass.; at far left, cupboard in the William Griswold House, Guilford, Conn.